SANTIAGO SAW THINGS DIFFERENTLY

Santiago Ramón y Cajal, Artist, Doctor, Father of Neuroscience

CHRISTINE IVERSON

illustrated by **LUCIANO LOZA**

> *Even when the work of a genius is subjected to critical analysis and no errors are found, it is important to realize that everything he has discovered in a particular field is almost nothing in comparison with what remains to be discovered. Nature offers inexhaustible wealth to all.*
> —Santiago Ramón y Cajal,
> *Advice for a Young Investigator*

☰ mit Kids Press

SANTIAGO'S grandfather had an ancient shop that hung on the craggy edge of the Spanish mountains. Inside were spools of itchy yarn and stone-still looms. It was a whispery place where only the dust moved.

But when Santiago visited the shop, he twirled and
tangled the woolen thread around his arms
and slid the wooden shuttles across
the floor. Dust sparkled and
soared in a kaleidoscope
of motion.

At home in his village, he played marro, he raced, he jumped, and he climbed.

He could turn old scraps of metal and wood into music and games.

By the time Santiago was eight, he had found a new way to move. Using a piece of chalk or charcoal, he swept lines and curves across doors, gates, and recently painted facades.

He drew bullfights, sinking ships, and ancient heroes with plumed helmets. To the neighbors, the drawings were a nuisance. But Santiago saw things differently. He was an artist . . . and always would be.

Santiago's father—the village doctor—thought art was a distraction. Santiago should be learning math, Latin, and strict discipline. But what if Santiago was as talented as the famous painter Velázquez? His father decided to find out.

He took Santiago and his best artwork to the village church, where a painter was whitewashing the walls. Santiago showed him his drawings. The painter frowned.
He shook his head.

"But," Santiago's father asked, "does the boy really show no aptitude for art?"

The painter frowned again. "None, my friend."

That settled it. To Santiago's father, who knew very little about art, the house painter's judgment was as good as any from a fine arts academy.

At home, Santiago's father delivered the final verdict. Santiago must study to become a doctor. He confiscated Santiago's paper and charcoal and pencils. No more distractions.

But to Santiago, drawing and painting were as natural and necessary as breathing. And his father hadn't found all his art supplies. So Santiago hid what he had left and drew in secret.

Once school started, Santiago covered the margins of his schoolbooks with drawings. When the teacher wasn't looking, the children passed the drawings around the room . . . until they were caught.

As punishment, the teacher locked Santiago in a dark basement room, but forgot to confiscate his pencil and paper. The room was lit by a wisp of light leaking through an old shutter— just enough light for drawing. Santiago stood atop a chair, pressed the paper to the ceiling, and drew for hours.

When Santiago turned ten, his parents sent him away to a religious school. The friars—his teachers—thought students should sit quietly, memorize, and recite. But not Santiago. He continued to cover the pages of his schoolbooks with drawings. And when he misbehaved, the friars confined him in the classroom until dinnertime. With no paper. So Santiago used his pencil to unlock the door.

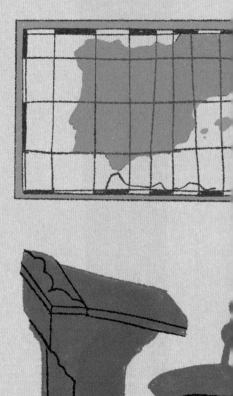

When Santiago was eleven, his parents chose a different school set against a backdrop of mountains, "leafy woodland paths," and "a paradise of butterflies and songbirds." As soon as his father's carriage departed, Santiago took the money meant for school supplies and bought his first paint box.

He brought his paint box on hikes, where he mixed green with blue to create olive trees, black with green to make cypress trees, yellow with green to make boxwood, and brown with black to make a cabin's frame. In his heart, he would always be an artist. But his father still wanted him to become a doctor.

One summer night, just before he turned sixteen, Santiago and his father slipped over a moonlit wall into an abandoned graveyard to find bits and pieces of skeletons.

They examined every detail of the bones. When Santiago fit the pieces

together like a puzzle, he "felt a special delight . . . in taking apart and putting together again, piece by piece, the organic clock." To Santiago's father, bones were a basic introduction to anatomy. But Santiago saw things differently. He saw the human body as a work of art.

He wanted to know more. At eighteen, he went to school in Zaragoza to study medicine. With lessons about the routes of arteries and the course of blood flow fresh in his mind, he explored the Ebro River.

He scrambled over rocks to follow it sliding through the mountains, curving around the cathedral, and finally flowing under a stone bridge.

After graduation, he had to trade hikes in the mountains for duty in Cuba with the Spanish Army. In Cuba, there were tropical forests, dangling vines, and swaying palm trees to explore. There was also malaria.

Santiago returned home too sick and weak to hike. Instead he used the last of his army pay to buy a microscope for studying anatomy. When he peered through the lens, he discovered a world rich with uncharted lands. He picked up his pencil and began to draw.

Santiago drew and studied and tutored until he became a professor of anatomy in Valencia.

In Valencia, Santiago learned about a problem. Other scientists couldn't understand exactly how people's brains worked. They knew nerve fibers—tiny, stringy structures—were involved, but nerve fibers were hard to see, even under a microscope. Some scientists tried to help by coloring the fibers with a stain. But the stain worked only on a few of the fibers.

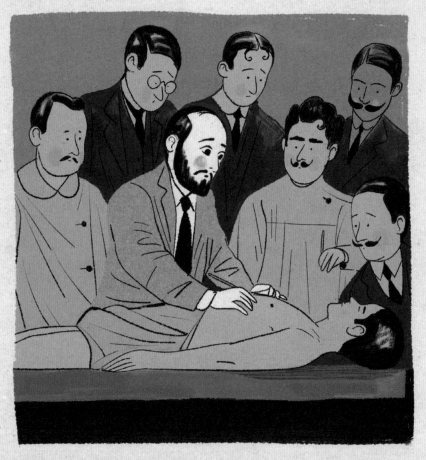

As for the rest of the fibers, they looked like a tangled forest, where the branches, vines, and thickets seemed interconnected in a never-ending web.

But Santiago saw things differently.

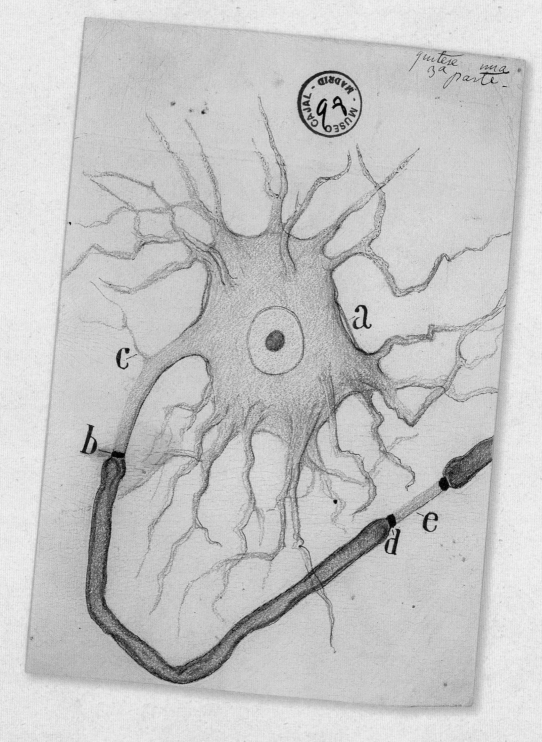

When Santiago looked through his microscope at the smallest and youngest of the fibers, he saw seeds, seedlings, and saplings. He drew pictures of the fibers at different stages of growth until his pencil began to unlock patterns.

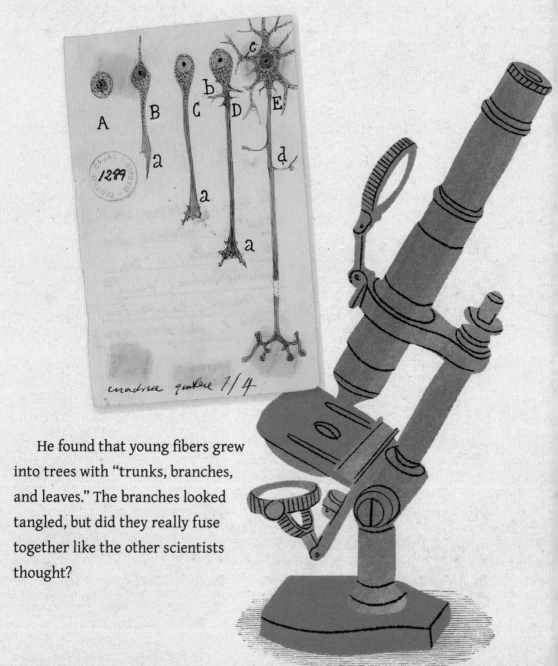

He found that young fibers grew into trees with "trunks, branches, and leaves." The branches looked tangled, but did they really fuse together like the other scientists thought?

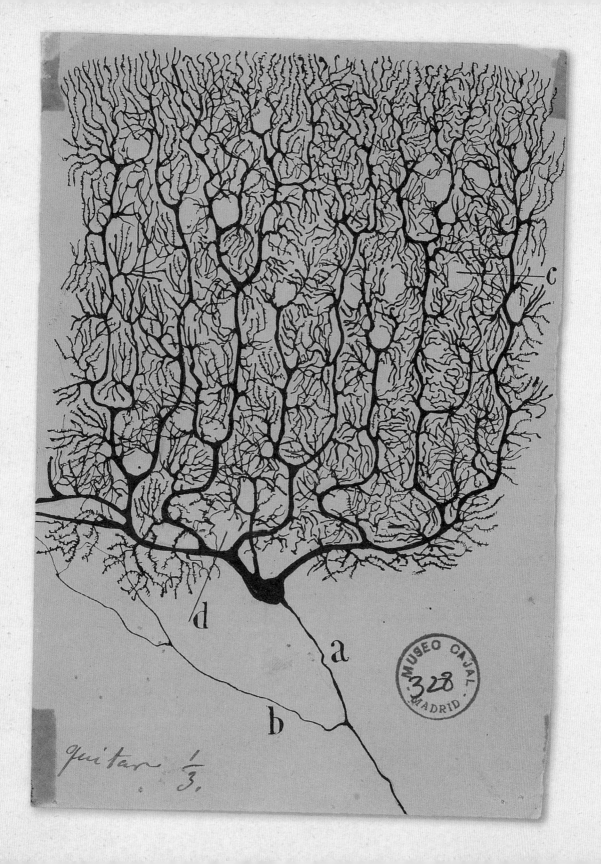

c

d

a

b

Santiago knew he would have to change the stain to see the branches more clearly. He experimented with different chemicals until he found just the right mixture. What he saw next took his breath away. The full-grown trees never fused together. They only reached out toward one another. The forest wasn't a tangled web. It was made up of individual trees!

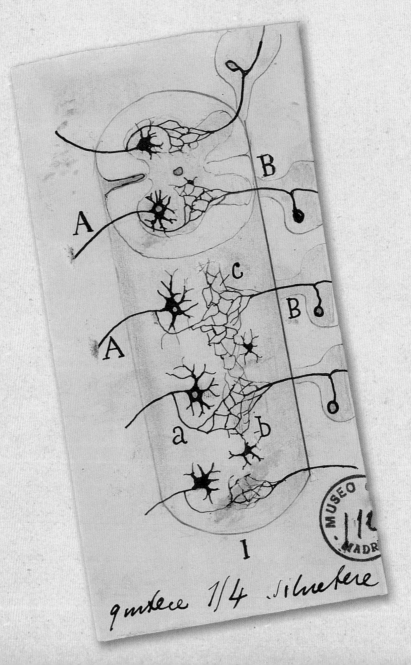

Once Santiago could see entire trees, he understood that he was looking at nerve cells separated by gaps. The more he drew, the more patterns he discovered.

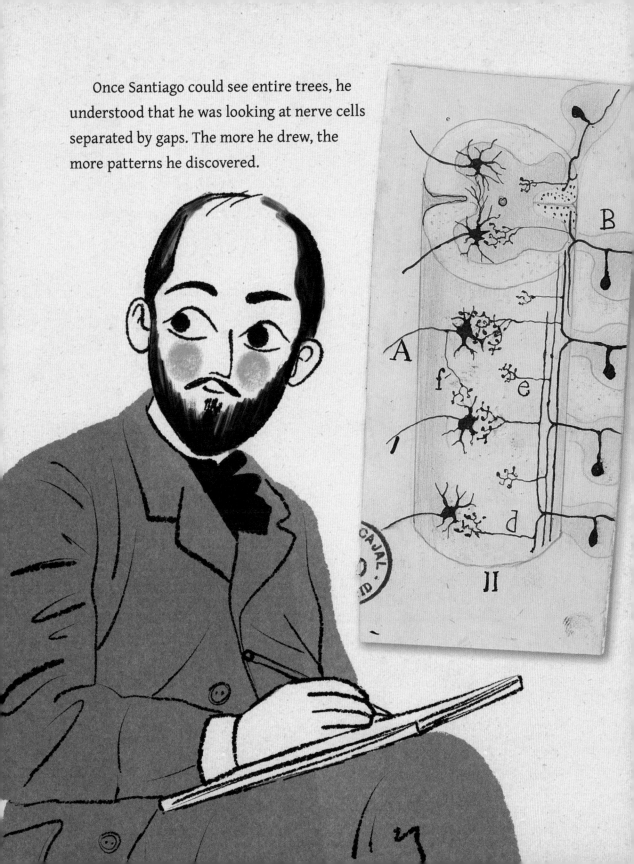

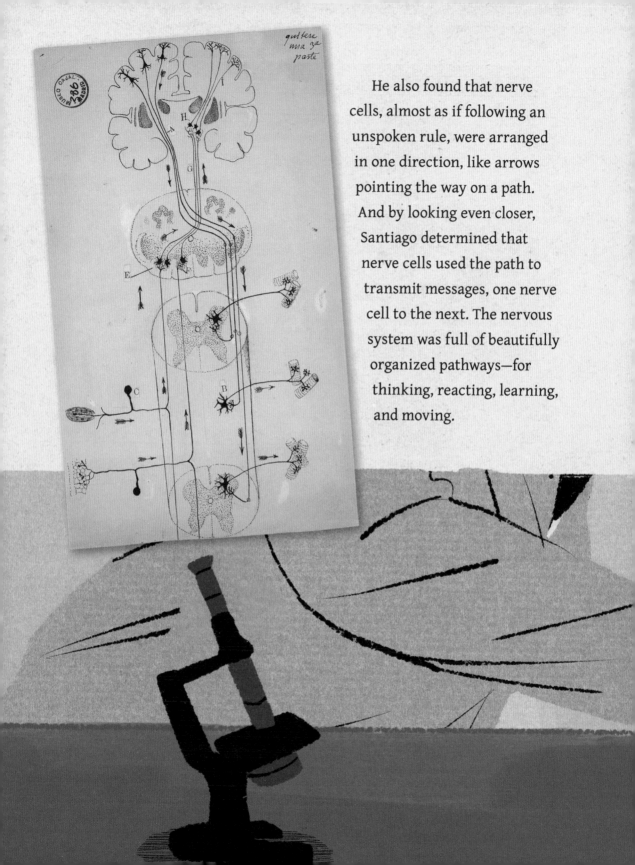

He also found that nerve cells, almost as if following an unspoken rule, were arranged in one direction, like arrows pointing the way on a path. And by looking even closer, Santiago determined that nerve cells used the path to transmit messages, one nerve cell to the next. The nervous system was full of beautifully organized pathways—for thinking, reacting, learning, and moving.

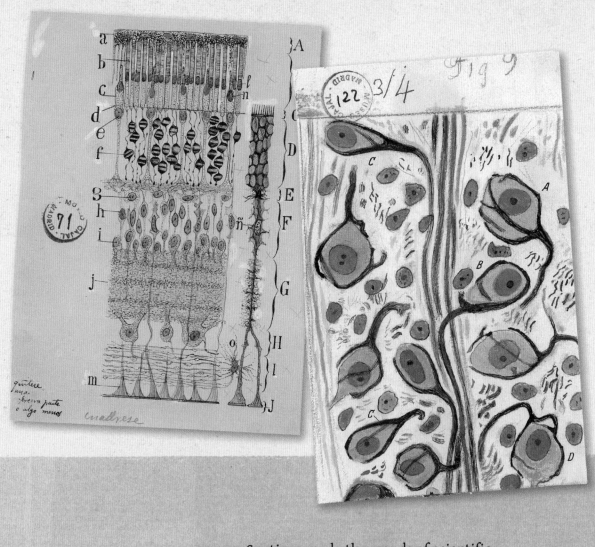

Santiago made thousands of scientific drawings—each one an intricate work of art. He sent his drawings all over the world and challenged other scientists until they could see, too. His work enabled scientists and doctors to find new ways to help people learn and heal.

Santiago changed the way scientists understood the nervous system because he saw things differently—brilliantly. With the eyes of an artist, he had found what he called the "mysterious butterflies of the soul," those tiny nerve cells that allow us to be a part of the world.

Santiago Ramón y Cajal became . . . the Father of Neuroscience.

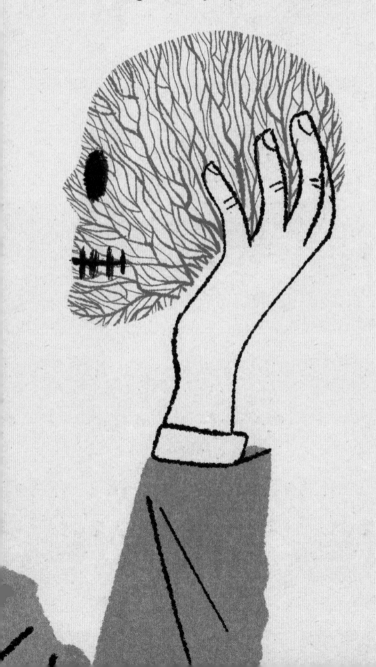

ANATOMY OF A NEURON

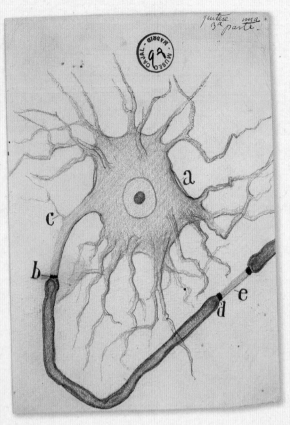

SANTIAGO WAS ABLE TO SEE AND DRAW the beauty within even the tiniest parts of nerve cells, now called neurons. Some of his scientific drawings are included in this book.

The three main parts of a neuron are the soma, the axon, and the dendrites. In the drawing at left, the soma (a) is the cell body. The axon (b) sends signals from the soma to other neurons. The dendrites (c) receive signals and carry them to the soma. Many axons have a coating, called myelin (d), and breaks in the coating, called nodes of Ranvier (e), that help speed the signal along the axon.

All cells, including neurons, have a control center inside the cell body called a nucleus. The image on the right is the nucleus of a pyramidal neuron from the cerebrum, in the brain. The part labeled (b) is a nucleolus, an organelle within the nucleus. The image below is a drawing of various types of nucleoli inside brain neuron nuclei (which are very tiny!).

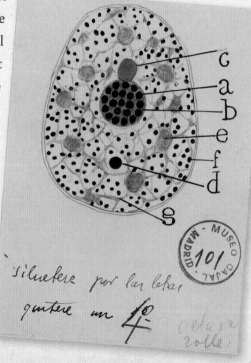

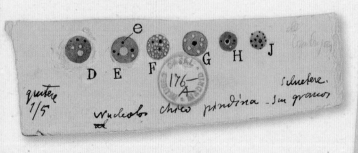

LIFE AND WORKS

SANTIAGO RAMÓN Y CAJAL'S breakthrough discovery is now known as the neuron doctrine: the neuron, or the nerve cell, is one distinct structure—an independent unit. Neurons pass information from one cell to the next using electrical or chemical signals.

When Santiago made his first discoveries in 1888, most scientists believed the nervous system was a continuous, interconnected web. But that theory didn't match up with their observations of how the nervous system worked. How could memories be both made and then also retrieved within a continuous web? How did the web grow when new information was learned? How could signals for both sensation (information in) and movement (action out) travel along the same web—and at the same time? Scientists were searching for answers.

Still, they didn't entirely believe Santiago's findings until they saw his drawings. For many scientists, that was the moment when the form and function of the nervous system snapped into focus. Several of the most accomplished and respected scientists in the world—like the anatomist Dr. Heinrich Wilhelm von Waldeyer, who coined the term "neuron" in 1891—enthusiastically supported Santiago and his neuron doctrine. It became the basis for modern-day neuroscience: the study of the structure and function of the nervous system, which includes the brain, the spinal cord, and all the nerves in the body (along with many supporting tissues).

In 1906, Santiago won the Nobel Prize for medicine. He shared the award with Dr. Camillo Golgi, the Italian scientist who invented the staining method Santiago used for his discoveries. Golgi still did not believe Santiago's findings and spent the majority of his Nobel Prize acceptance speech disagreeing with the neuron doctrine. Santiago was not flustered. The next day, he gave the speech he had planned, ignoring Golgi's criticism, crediting Golgi for inventing the staining method, and then explaining his own findings. By 1906, most scientists already supported Santiago's ideas, but Golgi spent the remainder of his lifetime believing his own theory, called the reticular theory, and rejecting the neuron doctrine. Scientists using modern technology have confirmed that Santiago was correct.

Santiago was also an avid photographer with experience altering chemical solutions, rinses, and exposure time to produce photographs using early cameras. He was one of the first Spanish photographers to take photos in color, and he used his photography knowledge to alter Golgi's stain and processes.

Always persistent and innovative, Santiago wasn't easily discouraged, even as a child. When his father forbade him from reading fiction, he found a secret rooftop perch that was perfect for storing and reading his favorites, including *Don Quixote*, *The Count of Monte Cristo*, and *Robinson Crusoe*. Throughout his lifetime, Santiago himself authored more than two hundred written works—scientific articles as well as books. Many of his books were about neuroscience, but he also wrote one of the first books about the science and art of color photography as well as five science fiction novels and a book called *Advice for a Young Investigator*, written for aspiring scientists.

In 1879, Santiago married Silveria Fañanás y García, and together they raised seven children. The Cajal family moved to Valencia and later Barcelona for

Santiago's job as a professor of anatomy and histology (microscopic anatomy). By 1900, they were living in Madrid, where Santiago had become the director of the National Institute of Hygiene. In 1901, he was named director of the Biological Research Laboratory in Madrid, known from 1920 on as the Cajal Institute. He continued to work there until his death in 1934 at the age of eighty-two.

CAMERA OBSCURA

The day Santiago found himself in the dark basement of his school with a pencil and a piece of paper, the pinhole opening in the shutters created a phenomenon called a camera obscura (*camera* means "room," *obscura* means "dark"). If the small basement window hadn't had shutters, white light would have filled the room. Instead, the beams of light coming through the pinhole created an exact replica of the scene outside—except upside down and backward. Light reflecting from the sky landed on the floor. Light reflecting from the square—the children playing and the horses walking—landed on the ceiling. It was as if Santiago were inside a life-size camera.

❧

SELECTED REFERENCES

Cajal, Santiago Ramón y. *Advice for a Young Investigator.* Translated by Neely Swanson and Larry W. Swanson. Cambridge, MA: The MIT Press, 2004.

Cajal, Santiago Ramón y. *Recollections of My Life.* Translated by E. Horne Craigie, with the assistance of Juan Cano. Cambridge, MA: The MIT Press, 1996. The quotations throughout the text are taken from this autobiography.

Swanson, Larry W., et al. *The Beautiful Brain: The Drawings of Santiago Ramón y Cajal.* New York: Abrams, 2017.

❧

Author **CHRISTINE IVERSON** has a doctoral degree in physical therapy and an MEd with a focus in children's literature. She first encountered Santiago Ramón y Cajal's work as a graduate student and was fascinated by his intricate artwork, his study of neuroscience, and his passionate approach to life. This is Christine Iverson's first book for children.

Illustrator **LUCIANO LOZANO** is an award-winning author and illustrator whose art is published in newspapers, magazines, and books, including *The Worst Sleepover in the World* by Sophie Dahl and *I (Don't) Like Snakes* by Nicola Davies. He lives in Barcelona.

For David, Jane, and Holly, who inspire me to see things differently,
and for Ben, who encourages me every step of the way —CI

To my sister Gloria —LL

———————

WITH SPECIAL THANKS to Ricardo Martínez Murillo, MD, PhD, director of the Cajal Institute in Madrid, Spain; Mónica Torrero at the Centro de Interpretación Santiago Ramón y Cajal in Ayerbe, Spain; Mark Zylka, PhD, at the University of North Carolina; and Eliot Dudik at the College of William and Mary.

———————

Text copyright © 2023 by Christine Iverson
Illustrations copyright © 2023 by Luciano Lozano
Art and photographs on pages 19, 22, 27–33, 36, 38, and back cover by Santiago Ramón y Cajal courtesy of the Cajal Institute, "Cajal Legacy," Spanish National Research Council (CSIC), Madrid, Spain

The MIT Press, the ☰mit Kids Press colophon, and MIT Kids Press are trademarks of The MIT Press, a department of the Massachusetts Institute of Technology, and used under license from The MIT Press. The colophon and MIT Kids Press are registered in the US Patent and Trademark Office.

First paperback edition 2024

Library of Congress Catalog Card Number 2022923366
ISBN 978-1-5362-2453-5 (English hardcover)
ISBN 978-1-5362-3833-4 (English paperback)
ISBN 978-1-5362-3334-6 (Spanish hardcover)
ISBN 978-1-5362-3964-5 (Spanish paperback)

24 25 26 27 28 29 CCP 10 9 8 7 6 5 4 3 2 1

Printed in Shenzhen, Guangdong, China

This book was typeset in Gentium Basic.
The illustrations were created digitally.

MIT Kids Press
an imprint of Candlewick Press
99 Dover Street
Somerville, Massachusetts 02144

mitkidspress.com
candlewick.com